AF480654

PATHWAYS TO PURPOSE

LIFE LESSONS FROM THE BHAGAVAD GITA FOR ASPIRING YOUNG MINDS

DR. MINAKSHI BANSAL

Made with ♥ on the Notion Press Platform
www.notionpress.com

DEDICATION

This book is dedicated to all the young souls on their journey to find purpose and meaning in life. May the timeless wisdom of the Bhagavad Gita light your path, inspire your heart, and strengthen your resolve to live with courage, compassion, and authenticity. May you find in these pages a source of strength and inspiration that guides you through both trials and triumphs, encouraging you to rise above challenges and embrace your highest potential.

ᐅᐅᐅ

Contents

Contents

Prayer

"Om Bhadram Karnebhih Shrinuyama Devah
Bhadram Pashyemakshabhiryajatrah
Sthirairangais Tushtuvamsastanubhih
Vyashema Devahitam Yadayuh
Svasti Na Indro Vriddhashravah
Svasti Nah Pusha Vishwavedah
Svasti Nastarkshyo Arishtanemih
Svasti No Brihaspatir Dadhatu
Om Shantih Shantih Shantih"

This mantra is a prayer for universal well-being, invoking the blessings of various deities for protection, health, and happiness. It emphasizes the importance of experiencing the auspicious through all senses and living a life aligned with divine purpose. The repetition of "Shantih" at the end signifies a deep desire for peace in the individual, the environment, and the universe at large. This mantra is often recited as a prayer for peace, prosperity, and the physical and spiritual well-being of all beings.

ᐁᐁᐁ

About The Author

Dr. Minakshi Bansal, born in the bustling metropolis of Delhi, India, has led a life steeped in artistry, scholarly pursuit, and an unwavering commitment to societal betterment. Following her marriage, she relocated to Ahmedabad, Gujarat, where she has since blossomed into a multifaceted beacon of inspiration for many. Dr. Minakshi is not only recognized as a gifted artist in the realm of Fine Arts but also as an esteemed author, a devoted social worker and a dedicated research scholar in Psychology. Her journey, marked by a profound dedication to elevating those around her, especially the downtrodden and underprivileged children of society, is a testament to her deep-seated belief in the transformative power of engagement and empathy.

From her earliest days, Minakshi was distinguished by an insatiable appetite for reading. Her literary universe was inhabited by characters and narratives that spanned ethical tales, motivational and inspirational stories, and the mythic parables imbued with life lessons. This voracious reading habit was not merely for personal edification but was driven by a desire to distill and disseminate the essence of these narratives to foster the development of students and peers alike. She was particularly captivated by the lives and teachings of historical figures and spiritual leaders such as Adi Shankaracharya, Swami Vivekananda, Dr. APJ Abdul Kalam, Mahamana Pandit Madan Mohan Malviya, Mahatma Gandhi, Sardar Vallabhai Patel, and Vinoba Bhave, among others. Their philosophies and life stories fueled her ambition to embody their ideals of resilience, selflessness, and relentless pursuit of knowledge.

Dr. Minakshi's academic and practical engagement with psychology has been equally noteworthy. As a research scholar, her focus has been on exploring the intricate tapestry of the human psyche, aiming to unlock the potential for psychological well-being and societal harmony. Her scholarly work is complemented by her active involvement in social work, where she employs her academic insights to make tangible differences in the lives of the underprivileged. Her endeavours in social work are characterized by an innovative approach that combines traditional wisdom with contemporary psychological practices to address the multifaceted challenges faced by these communities.

Her artistic talents, another facet of her diverse capabilities, are not merely a personal passion but also serve as a medium through which she communicates and connects with others. Her art, rich in symbolism and emotional depth, reflects her philosophical inquiries and social concerns, offering viewers a glimpse into the breadth of her intellect and the depth of her compassion.

In addition to her contributions to the arts and social sciences, Dr. Minakshi has embraced the healing arts of Pranic Healing, mastering the techniques developed by Master Choa Kok Sui. This practice, which focuses on the manipulation of Prana or life energy to heal the body and aura, has been both a personal journey of discovery and a means through which she extends her healing touch to others. Her proficiency in Pranic Healing is complemented by her advocacy and teaching of various forms of meditation aimed at rejuvenation, personal betterment, and the cultivation of harmony within individuals and communities alike.

Dr. Minakshi's life is a narrative of relentless pursuit, not just of personal achievement but of the upliftment and empowerment of society at large. Her diverse interests and talents—spanning the arts, literature, psychology, and the healing practices—converge on a singular path of service. She embodies the spirit of the luminaries who inspired her, channelling their legacy through her actions and teachings. Through her books, art, and social initiatives, she continues to inspire a new generation to embark on their own journeys of self-discovery, resilience, and altruism.

Her commitment to social betterment, particularly her focus on uplifting underprivileged children, reflects a deep understanding of the transformative potential of education and personal development. By integrating her knowledge of psychology, her artistic sensibilities, and her healing practices, Dr. Bansal has developed a holistic approach to social work that addresses both the immediate needs and the long-term well-being of the communities she serves.

As an author, Dr. Minakshi's writings offer a blend of inspirational insights, practical wisdom, and reflective contemplations drawn from her extensive reading and life experiences. Her books serve as a guide for those seeking to navigate the complexities of life with grace, resilience, and purpose. Through her narratives, she extends an invitation to her readers to explore the depths of their own potential and to contribute meaningfully to the collective well-being of society.

In Dr. Minakshi Bansal, we find a remarkable synthesis of the artist, the scholar, the healer, and the social activist. Her life's work stands as a beacon of hope and a source of inspiration for individuals seeking to make a difference in the world. Her story is a compelling reminder of the power of individual action, rooted in compassion and driven by a profound commitment to the betterment of humanity. Dr. Minakshi's legacy is not just in the tangible outcomes of her efforts but in the enduring spirit of inquiry, empathy, and service that she embodies.

ᑭᑭᑭ

Preface

In this book, we embark on a journey of exploration into one of the world's oldest and most revered spiritual texts, the Bhagavad Gita. The teachings of the Gita are profound and vast, offering guidance on how to navigate the complexities of life with grace, courage, and wisdom. It is a guide that has the potential to transform not only individual lives but also the very fabric of society. My aim in writing this book has been to distill the essence of these timeless teachings and present them in a manner that resonates with young minds aspiring to lead a life of purpose and fulfillment.

The Bhagavad Gita, set in the epic Mahabharata, unfolds in the form of a dialogue between Prince Arjuna and his charioteer, Lord Krishna, on the battlefield of Kurukshetra. At first glance, the setting might seem too distant from the contemporary challenges faced by today's youth. However, the psychological and spiritual dilemmas faced by Arjuna are universal and enduring, touching upon the fundamental questions about duty, righteousness, and the search for meaning—questions that are incredibly pertinent to the modern world.

The Gita does not offer mere solutions but rather provides the tools to enhance understanding and judgment, empowering one to make decisions that are aligned with one's deeper values and aspirations. It teaches us about the importance of duty (dharma), the qualities of effective leadership, the need for self-control, and the power of detachment from the results of our actions. These lessons are invaluable for anyone who is navigating the transition from youth to adulthood, where decisions have far-reaching implications on the future.

In this book, each chapter delves into a specific teaching of the Gita, drawing out life lessons that are both practical and spiritually enriching. I have endeavored to present these teachings in a context that is relatable and applicable to the everyday lives of young readers. Whether it's dealing with academic pressure, making career choices, handling relationships, or developing a sense of identity and self-worth, the Gita's insights are immensely relevant.

Moreover, the Gita's call to perform one's duty with dedication and integrity, without attachment to the fruits of one's actions, offers a powerful antidote to the modern-day stresses associated with success and achievement. It teaches balance and offers a broader perspective on success, one that includes spiritual growth and personal well-being.

One of the most compelling aspects of the Gita is its emphasis on self-realization—the discovery and fulfillment of one's true potential. This book explores this theme extensively, offering guidance on how to align one's actions with one's innermost values and aspirations. The journey of self-realization is not about finding a fixed destination but about continual growth and understanding, qualities that are essential in today's rapidly changing world.

Additionally, this book addresses the concept of karma (action) and dharma (righteousness) in the context of personal and professional life. Understanding these concepts can help young individuals make choices that are not only good for them but are also aligned with the greater good of their communities and the world at large.

The teachings of the Bhagavad Gita also extend to leadership and the responsibilities that come with it. In a world that increasingly values authenticity and integrity in leaders, the Gita's emphasis on leading by example, with wisdom and compassion, is particularly relevant. It offers a model of leadership that is not about asserting power but about empowering others—a vital lesson for anyone who aspires to be a leader in their field.

Finally, this book is an invitation to reflect, question, and discover one's path to purpose. It encourages readers to engage actively with the teachings of the Gita, not as passive recipients of wisdom but as active participants in a dialogue with themselves about their life's direction and purpose.

My hope is that this book serves as a companion on your journey, offering insights that illuminate and inspire. May the lessons of the Gita guide you to live with greater awareness, purpose, and joy, helping you to navigate life's challenges with confidence and grace.

Dr. Minakshi Bansal
Social Activist
Ahmedabad, Gujarat, Bharat

ONE

DISCOVERING YOUR PATH

The Bhagavad Gita, often referred to as the Gita, is a 700-verse Hindu scripture that is part of the Indian epic Mahabharata. It consists of a conversation between Prince Arjuna and the god Krishna, who serves as his charioteer. This sacred text is revered for its profound wisdom and spiritual guidance, offering lessons that extend far beyond the confines of ancient warfare and into the intricacies of human motivations and actions. It has been studied not just for religious reasons but as a guide to navigating the complex challenges of life.

One of the most significant aspects of the Gita is its ability to present deep philosophical insights in a manner that is accessible and applicable to everyday life. For young minds especially, the Gita serves as a beacon of wisdom, guiding them through the turbulent phases of growth and self-discovery. It helps in answering fundamental questions about duty, purpose, morality, and the pursuit of success, which are particularly pertinent during one's formative years.

At its core, the Gita encourages readers to find their path to self-realization and to understand the nature of the world and their place within it. It prompts a journey of internal reflection where one can confront their deepest fears and desires, thereby enabling them to act with wisdom and confidence. This process of self-reflection is crucial for personal development, as it helps young individuals to develop a sense of identity and purpose that is not swayed by external pressures or fleeting emotions.

The conversation between Krishna and Arjuna begins on the battlefield of Kurukshetra, where Arjuna is filled with doubt and moral dilemma about fighting in the war against his own relatives, beloved friends, and revered teachers. In this context, Krishna imparts spiritual enlightenment and practical advice to Arjuna, illuminating the paths of righteousness and the nature of life and death. This discourse encourages the young reader to consider their duties in the world and how they can be fulfilled in alignment with their personal values and societal responsibilities.

Krishna's counsel in the Gita transcends the immediate context of the battlefield, offering guidance on how to balance material responsibilities and spiritual growth. He introduces the concept of 'dharma' or duty, which is central to understanding one's purpose in life. For the youth, deciphering one's dharma can be particularly challenging, yet the Gita provides a framework for how to approach these duties with dedication and without attachment to the outcomes, a principle known as 'Nishkama Karma.'

The Gita also delves into various paths (yogas) towards achieving spiritual realization and integrating them into daily life. These include Karma Yoga (the yoga of selfless action), Bhakti Yoga (the path of devotion), and Jnana Yoga (the path of knowledge). Each of these paths offers unique insights and practices that can help individuals cultivate discipline, compassion, and wisdom—qualities that are essential for any young person navigating the complexities of modern life.

Moreover, the Gita's discussion on the nature of self (Atman) and the universe (Brahman) invites young minds to explore the deeper philosophical questions about existence and the eternal spirit. Understanding these concepts can lead to profound transformations in how one perceives their life and the lives of others, fostering a sense of connectedness and universal responsibility.

For young individuals looking to forge a meaningful life path, the Gita provides invaluable lessons on resilience and the importance of maintaining one's moral compass in the face of challenges. It teaches that true success is achieved not merely through the accumulation of wealth or accolades but through the pursuit of knowledge, the performance of duty, and the cultivation of virtue.

The Bhagavad Gita's timeless wisdom is incredibly relevant for today's youth, offering both practical advice and profound spiritual insights. It encourages an introspective approach to life's challenges, promoting a balanced perspective that values duty, morality, and personal growth. As young individuals strive to make their mark in the world, the Gita serves as a guiding light, helping them to discover their path and navigate it with courage, integrity, and purpose. By internalizing the lessons of the Gita, they can not only achieve personal fulfillment but also contribute positively to the world around them.

▷▷▷

"The journey of self-discovery inspired by the Bhagavad Gita teaches us that our true strength lies not in the might of arms but in the resolve of the spirit. When faced with life's battles, look within to find your courage and clarity. Your inner self holds the wisdom to navigate the complexities of life."

❦❦❦

TWO
THE DILEMMA OF DUTY

The opening scene of the Bhagavad Gita presents a poignant picture of Arjuna, a great warrior, standing on the battlefield of Kurukshetra, overcome with doubt and moral uncertainty. This moment is not just a physical confrontation but also a deep psychological and ethical crisis. Arjuna, torn between his duties as a warrior and his love for his relatives on the opposing side, faces a dilemma that goes to the core of human existence: the conflict between the demands of one's role in society and the dictates of one's heart.

Arjuna's chariot stands between two armies, ready for battle, but he is paralyzed by sorrow and compassion, unable to move forward. He sees his respected elders, beloved friends, and close relatives on both sides, ready to fight each other. The prospect of killing his kith and kin for the sake of a kingdom and pleasure deeply disturbs him. Arjuna questions the moral justification of the war and the resulting destruction of family structures, which he believes would lead to societal chaos and spiritual downfall. His bow, Gandiva, slips from his hand as his mind is consumed with grief and confusion.

In response to Arjuna's profound distress, Krishna, his charioteer and guide, delivers a discourse that addresses the fundamental aspects of duty, righteousness, and the nature of life and death. Krishna's teachings in the Gita are not merely instructions to a despondent soldier but are universal principles meant to guide individuals through the complexities of life's battles.

Krishna begins by challenging Arjuna's understanding of life and death. He explains that the soul (Atman) is eternal—it neither kills nor can be killed. The physical body is merely temporary, and death is just a passage into another form. This perspective is meant to fortify Arjuna against the immediate emotional pain of his actions by focusing on the broader, spiritual view of life.

As the discourse progresses, Krishna elaborates on the concept of 'dharma,' or rightful duty. For Arjuna, his dharma as a warrior is to fight for justice and protect the righteous. Krishna argues that shirking his duty would be dishonorable and detrimental to his spiritual journey. He introduces the idea of 'Nishkama Karma'—action without attachment to outcomes, where duties are performed according to one's role in society, without any selfish desire for the results. This principle encourages individuals to engage fully in their responsibilities while remaining detached from the success or failure of their actions.

Krishna's counsel to Arjuna extends beyond the battlefield, offering a framework for dealing with ethical dilemmas in personal and professional life. He emphasizes the importance of intention and motivation in performing one's duty. Actions aligned with one's dharma, performed without selfish motives, lead to spiritual purity and societal harmony.

The lesson from this initial chapter of the Gita resonates strongly with young individuals today, who may find themselves at crossroads, facing tough choices in personal and professional spheres. It teaches that integrity involves recognizing and fulfilling one's duties, even when they conflict with personal desires or social pressures. It encourages a balanced approach to duty, where one's actions are guided by a deeper understanding of one's role and responsibilities.

This balance is not easily achieved and requires deep introspection and a clear understanding of one's values and goals. The Gita does not dismiss the emotional turmoil that often accompanies difficult decisions but instead offers a way to navigate these emotions with wisdom and clarity.

In practical terms, applying the lesson of the Dilemma of Duty means cultivating the ability to make decisions that are ethically sound and aligned with one's deeper purpose, regardless of the immediate emotional discomfort these decisions may cause. It means building a character that is resilient in the face of personal and professional challenges, and that prioritizes the greater good over transient, personal gains.

The dialogue between Krishna and Arjuna thus sets the stage for a profound exploration of life's moral complexities. It encourages young individuals to seek a deeper understanding of their purpose and duties, and to act with integrity and courage, even when faced with the most daunting challenges.

As individuals strive to navigate their personal and professional lives with integrity, the teachings of the Gita provide valuable insights into managing conflicts and making choices that are not only right for oneself but also for the larger community. It underscores the importance of ethical conduct and moral courage, qualities that are essential for any individual seeking to lead a purposeful and impactful life.

॥ॐॐ॥

"In every decision lies the potential for growth and the echo of eternity. Let your choices not just serve the moment but also align with the timeless virtues of righteousness and truth. The Gita teaches us that true success is measured not by outcomes but by the purity of our actions."

▷▷▷

THREE

THE PHILOSOPHY OF ACTION

The second chapter of the Bhagavad Gita, often regarded as its philosophical core, introduces the profound concept of 'Karma Yoga'—the path of selfless action. This principle is fundamental to understanding the Gita's approach to life and fulfillment, providing crucial insights into how actions can be performed in a manner that leads to spiritual liberation and worldly success, without the entrapments of personal gain or loss.

The setting remains the battlefield where Arjuna, laden with doubt and confusion about engaging in the war, seeks guidance from Krishna. Here, Krishna broadens the conversation from addressing Arjuna's immediate dilemma to exploring the broader implications of action and duty in life. Krishna explains that one must learn to act according to their dharma (duty) without attachment to the results of those actions.

This philosophy is not merely about indifference or lack of engagement; rather, it is about a deep commitment to action, but with an equanimity that transcends the dualities of success and failure, joy and sorrow.

Krishna tells Arjuna that he has the right to perform his prescribed duties but should remain indifferent to the fruits of actions. This teaching is encapsulated in the famous verse: "You have a right to perform your prescribed duties, but you are not entitled to the fruits of your actions." This perspective is meant to cultivate a mindset where the focus is on the action itself and not on the outcome, which can lead to either ego inflation with success or discouragement with failure.

The concept of selfless action, or Nishkama Karma, is revolutionary in its simplicity and profundity. It suggests that true fulfillment in life does not come from what we acquire or achieve but from the purity of our actions. By detaching from the outcomes of our actions, we free ourselves from the constant oscillations of happiness and distress that accompany our attachments to specific results.

This detachment is not a form of disengagement from the world; rather, it's an engaged neutrality where one is fully involved in the world but not of it.

Krishna further expounds that this philosophy is not just applicable to the battlefield but is relevant to all facets of life. Whether one is a student, a professional, or a homemaker, the principle of performing one's duty with diligence but without attachment to the results can transform mundane daily activities into a spiritual practice.

This approach helps in developing a sense of inner peace and steadiness, which is essential for navigating the ups and downs of life.

In practical terms, applying the philosophy of action involves recognizing the deeper value of our duties and embracing them as opportunities for personal and spiritual growth. For instance, a student might focus on the process of learning with curiosity and diligence, rather than just on the grades; a professional might aim to contribute positively to their workplace and society, rather than solely chasing promotions or accolades.

This philosophy also teaches resilience and perseverance. By focusing on the effort rather than the outcome, one is less likely to get discouraged by setbacks or failures. Instead, every experience becomes a learning opportunity, a step in the journey of growth. This mindset is crucial for young individuals who are often faced with competitive pressures and fear of failure.

Moreover, the teaching of Karma Yoga promotes a sense of connectedness and responsibility towards others. When actions are performed with a consciousness of the welfare of others, rather than for personal gain, it fosters a spirit of service and community. This shift in perspective—from self-centeredness to selflessness—can lead to a more harmonious and compassionate society.

Krishna's discourse in this chapter reaches its climax with the introduction of the concept of 'sthitaprajna'—the man of steady wisdom. This ideal state is characterized by a person who remains unperturbed in success and failure, and who sees alike pleasure and pain. Achieving this state requires practice and detachment, as it involves rising above the dualities that normally disturb the human mind.

In the contemporary world, where action is often measured by its visible outcomes, the Gita's emphasis on intention and effort provides a refreshing counterpoint. It encourages a holistic approach to action—where the quality and ethics of one's actions are as important as, if not more than, the outcomes.

This wisdom is not only a route to personal peace and fulfillment but also a foundational principle for creating a just and sustainable world.

The philosophy of action as presented in the Bhagavad Gita offers a transformative approach to life's endeavors. By embracing the path of selfless action, individuals can navigate the complexities of life with grace and equanimity, achieving true fulfillment while contributing positively to the world around them.

༤༤༤

"*Embrace duty as a path to spiritual awakening and personal fulfillment. The Gita reminds us that duty performed without attachment to results purifies the soul, freeing us from the shackles of ego. In this selfless service, we find our deepest joy and our true purpose.*"

❧❧❧

FOUR

THE POWER OF WILL

The third chapter of the Bhagavad Gita delves into the practical application of the teachings discussed in earlier sections, focusing specifically on Karma Yoga—the yoga of action—and how it intersects with the human will. This chapter emphasizes the critical role of willpower and commitment in the pursuit of life goals, underpinning the notion that true success is achieved through disciplined action driven by a resolute will.

Krishna begins by reiterating the importance of action in human life. He clarifies that no one can remain actionless even for a moment; everyone is driven to act by the qualities born of nature. The essential message here is the inevitability of action which, when guided by willpower and commitment, can lead to higher spiritual and worldly achievements. Krishna counsels Arjuna on the need to perform his duties efficiently and without attachment to the results, which is the essence of Karma Yoga.

In explaining the dynamics of action and will, Krishna distinguishes between actions performed out of desire and those carried out from a sense of duty. The latter, he argues, are superior because they are not tied to personal gain and are more likely to lead to purity of mind and satisfaction. This teaching underscores the value of willpower as the driving force behind such dutiful action. When willpower aligns with dharma (duty), it helps an individual overcome the inertia of inaction and the impulsive motivations driven by personal desires.

The Gita's discussion about willpower extends to controlling the senses, which are often the greatest impediments to effective action. Krishna uses the metaphor of the tortoise, which withdraws its limbs into its shell, to describe how one should control the senses. Just as the tortoise controls its limbs, individuals should exercise control over their senses and direct their actions by a strong will, focused on their duties. This control is not about suppression but about redirection of energy from the pursuit of sense gratifications to more meaningful objectives aligned with one's life goals and duties.

This brings to light another critical aspect of willpower—its role in managing internal conflicts. Krishna explains how the senses, the mind, and the intellect are the sites of this battle and how one must strengthen the intellect to govern the mind and the senses. This hierarchy underlines the progression from mere control of impulses to the development of discernment and wisdom, which are necessary for making informed, ethical decisions. Therefore, strengthening willpower is not only about resisting temptations but also about empowering oneself with the ability to discern right from wrong and act accordingly.

The power of will is also discussed in the context of societal roles and responsibilities. Krishna tells Arjuna that even people of achievement, such as kings and sages, are bound by their inherent duties. He stresses that actions performed in alignment with one's societal role can lead to great achievements, provided they are driven by a strong will and commitment to duty. This is illustrated through the example of Janaka, the king-sage, who attained perfection solely through performance of prescribed duties.

Furthermore, Krishna addresses the contagious nature of action driven by a strong will. He advises Arjuna to set an example for others, as people follow the leaders of their societies. Here, the power of will transcends individual action and enters the domain of leadership. Effective leaders inspire others not just through their words but through their commitment and disciplined actions. This aspect of willpower is crucial for anyone aspiring to influence and lead others—be it in a family, community, or a larger social context.

The teachings of the Gita about the power of will and action culminate in the argument that every action, when performed with commitment and willpower, has the potential to become a means of spiritual liberation. By acting selflessly, with a focus on duty rather than personal gain, individuals can transcend the binding effects of their actions and move towards spiritual growth.

In practical terms, this means that young individuals should cultivate their willpower through regular practice, disciplined living, and a focus on higher goals. This cultivation involves understanding one's duties, aligning actions with these duties, and performing them with an unwavering commitment. Such a disciplined approach not only brings success in worldly terms but also contributes to inner growth and stability.

In essence, the Gita's teachings on the power of will and commitment offer a comprehensive framework for achieving life goals. They provide guidance on harnessing one's energies and directing them towards meaningful and dutiful actions, which lead to personal and spiritual fulfillment. As individuals navigate their lives, incorporating these teachings can help them achieve a harmonious balance between their desires, duties, and ultimate life aspirations.

ᗰᗰᗰ

"Leadership, as taught by the Gita, is about
nurturing and empowering, not controlling or
dominating. True leaders inspire trust and foster
strength in others by their example of integrity and
compassion. They know that leading is serving, and
in service, we find greatness."

༅༅༅

FIVE

The Path of Wisdom

The Bhagavad Gita's fourth chapter serves as a profound exploration into the nature of knowledge and wisdom, emphasizing their essential roles in guiding one towards enlightened choices and a meaningful life. Here, the text expands upon earlier discussions by delving into the intricacies of Jnana Yoga, or the path of wisdom, which underscores the transformative power of knowledge in spiritual and practical realms.

Krishna begins by recounting the divine origin of the teachings he imparts to Arjuna, explaining how this ancient wisdom has been transmitted through generations. He emphasizes the purity and sanctity of this knowledge, underscoring its importance as a tool for liberation. Krishna's historical recounting serves not only to authenticate the teachings but also to illustrate the cyclical and perennial nature of wisdom.

At the heart of this chapter is the principle that true wisdom transcends mere intellectual understanding; it is an experiential knowledge that permeates one's being and transforms one's actions. Krishna distinguishes between knowledge that is theoretical and wisdom that is practical and applied, stressing that the latter leads to self-realization and enlightenment. He argues that actions based on wisdom are more effective and purifying than those based merely on ritualistic practices or material gains.

Krishna further expounds on the different types of knowledge and the importance of approaching wisdom through humility and sincerity. He speaks of the value of learning from those who are wise, advocating for a mentorship approach where knowledge is not simply absorbed but experienced through service, inquiry, and a deep respect for the teacher. This relationship between the student and the teacher is portrayed as sacred and crucial in the journey towards wisdom.

The discourse then shifts to the concept of 'sacrifice'—a term broadly interpreted in the Gita. Krishna broadens the traditional notion of sacrifice as ritualistic offerings to include any action that is done with sincerity, dedication, and purity of purpose. This redefinition invites individuals to consider all actions as potential offerings to the divine, provided they are performed with the right attitude and wisdom. By doing so, every mundane activity is transformed into a spiritual practice, and this act of sanctification through wisdom leads to personal and collective elevation.

The transformative power of wisdom is further emphasized through its ability to clarify and purify. Krishna asserts that in the blazing fire of knowledge, all actions are purified. This metaphor highlights wisdom as a powerful force that burns away ignorance, doubt, and misconception, allowing one to see things as they truly are. This clarity is essential for making enlightened choices—decisions that are aligned with one's higher self and the universal good.

Furthermore, Krishna discusses the impact of wisdom on liberation, stating that nothing in this world purifies like wisdom. Once attained, it guides the individual directly to the supreme goal.

This path of wisdom is described as one of gradual awakening, where each step taken in knowledge leads to greater clarity and closer proximity to the divine.

As the narrative unfolds, Krishna also addresses the barriers to wisdom, such as doubt, and provides guidance on overcoming these through decisive action and firm faith. He warns Arjuna against the paralyzing effects of doubt, which can destroy one's moral fiber and spiritual progress. Here, wisdom is portrayed not only as a body of knowledge to be acquired but also as a proactive and dynamic process of engagement with the world.

In practical terms, the teachings of this chapter have profound implications for how individuals, especially young people, can approach life's decisions. In an age characterized by information overload, distinguishing between information, knowledge, and wisdom becomes crucial. Wisdom involves the ability to apply knowledge in ways that are ethical, beneficial, and harmonious. This application is what shapes a meaningful life, guiding individuals to act with consideration for the wider consequences of their actions on themselves and others.

By embracing the path of wisdom, as elucidated in the Gita, individuals learn to navigate the complexities of life with discernment and grace. They are equipped to make choices that not only serve their immediate interests but also contribute to their ultimate purpose and well-being. This chapter, thus, serves as a vital guide for anyone seeking to live a life defined by enlightened choices, urging a journey through knowledge towards the profound shores of wisdom and understanding. Through this journey, life becomes not just an accumulation of experiences but a deliberate and thoughtful voyage towards fulfillment and enlightenment.

ppp

"Every challenge is an invitation to strengthen our character and deepen our understanding. The Gita shows us that difficulties are not obstacles but opportunities to demonstrate our commitment to our values. Stand firm in adversity, and let your spirit be unshaken."

ᐯᐯᐯ

SIX

THE DISCIPLINE OF RENUNCIATION

The Bhagavad Gita, in its fifth chapter, introduces a compelling discourse on the discipline of renunciation, illustrating how the relinquishment of ego and selfish desires can catalyze a journey towards inner peace and purposeful living. This profound teaching navigates through the complexities of renunciation, not merely as an act of giving up but as a conscious choice to transcend the ego and its associated attachments.

Renunciation, or Sannyasa in the traditional sense, has often been misunderstood as the mere abandonment of worldly possessions and social obligations. However, the Gita refines this concept, portraying it as an internal state of detachment from the fruits of one's actions, rather than a physical abandonment of activity. This elevated understanding of renunciation shifts the focus from external renouncement to a more challenging and meaningful internal conquest—the conquest of the ego.

The ego, as addressed in the Gita, is the individual's identification with the self as separate from others and the rest of the universe. It is this sense of 'I' and 'mine' that binds a person to their desires, leading to actions that aim primarily at personal gain and consequently, to the inevitable fluctuations of joy and sorrow. Krishna, through his dialogue with Arjuna, emphasizes that true peace and purpose are not attainable through the fulfillment of these desires but through the dissolution of the ego that fuels them.

To dissolve the ego, one must practice Karma Yoga, the path of selfless action. This involves performing one's duties without any attachment to the outcomes—whether success or failure, gain or loss. By aligning one's actions with duty and a broader sense of service to others, without the egoistic desire for personal reward, one cultivates an inner purity and a state of equanimity. This state is crucial for the mind to transcend the dualities of life, such as pleasure and pain, which are often sources of psychological turmoil.

Krishna further elaborates on the concept of renunciation in action, which is more challenging and spiritually profound than renunciation in withdrawal. To renounce in action is to engage fully in the responsibilities and activities of the world, yet remain untethered to the ego's demands and expectations. This form of renunciation is dynamic and practical, suitable for anyone regardless of their stage in life or social obligations. It suggests that true sannyasa is not about escaping life's duties but embracing them with a spirit of dedication and selflessness.

The strength of this approach lies in its ability to transform everyday activities into a spiritual practice. When actions are performed as offerings to the divine, without selfish attachment, they become a means of purifying the heart and mind. This purification is essential for the development of discernment (viveka) and dispassion (vairagya), qualities that are indispensable for spiritual growth and the realization of one's true nature.

Moreover, the discipline of renunciation brings clarity to one's purpose in life. By shedding the layers of egoistic desires and societal expectations, one can perceive their unique role in the larger cosmic play. This clarity empowers individuals to act with greater conviction and purpose, aligned not with self-centered goals but with the welfare of the community and the world at large.

Krishna reassures that this path of renounced action is not devoid of joy. On the contrary, it leads to a deeper, more stable form of happiness that does not depend on external circumstances. This joy springs from the serenity of being in harmony with one's deeper self and the universe, a state where the ego no longer dictates one's sense of self-worth or fulfillment.

In practical terms, embracing the discipline of renunciation means cultivating mindfulness in daily life. It involves observing one's thoughts and actions to recognize the influence of the ego and gradually learning to let go of those ego-driven impulses. This practice enhances one's emotional and mental resilience, as it reduces dependency on external validation and the need to control outcomes.

The teachings of the Gita on renunciation are particularly relevant in the contemporary world, where the pursuit of material success and recognition often leads to stress and dissatisfaction. By understanding and practicing the principles of renunciation, individuals can lead more balanced and fulfilling lives, marked by a profound sense of peace and purpose.

Ultimately, the journey of renunciation is a transformative process that not only liberates the individual from the bondage of the ego but also contributes to the creation of a more compassionate and self-aware society. It is a path that leads to the realization of one's highest potential, where actions are guided by wisdom and compassion, and life is lived in a state of grace and gratitude.

ppp

"Cultivate a mind that sees the unity in diversity, recognizing the divine spark in all beings. The Gita teaches that respect for life in all its forms is a reflection of our respect for the divine. Such reverence fosters compassion and a profound sense of connectedness with the world."

ᐅᐅᐅ

SEVEN

The Journey of Meditation

The sixth chapter of the Bhagavad Gita delves into the practice and philosophy of meditation, presenting it as an essential technique for achieving self-discovery and inner peace. This chapter offers a comprehensive guide on how to integrate meditation into one's life, underscoring its transformative potential not only as a practice of mind but as a pathway to spiritual realization.

Meditation, as described in the Gita, involves much more than the mere act of sitting quietly. It is an expansive practice that engages the mind, body, and spirit in a quest for self-mastery and enlightenment. Krishna, in his dialogue with Arjuna, outlines a detailed methodology for meditation, emphasizing its significance in achieving a state of deep inner peace and connecting with the divine essence within.

The process of meditation begins with the proper preparation of one's environment and self. Krishna advises finding a clean and secluded spot, where one can sit steadily on a firm seat that is neither too high nor too low. This physical setup is crucial as it influences the meditator's ability to maintain a stable posture and a focused mind. The environment should be conducive to tranquility and free from distractions, aiding the practitioner in achieving deeper levels of concentration.

Once the external setup is addressed, the focus shifts to the posture and the body. The meditator is instructed to sit with a straight spine, keeping the body, head, and neck aligned and still. The eyes should gently close, with the gaze directed slightly upwards towards the center of the forehead, a technique aimed at facilitating concentration. This physical alignment is vital as it not only prevents physical discomfort but also promotes the flow of energy within the body, which is essential for effective meditation.

With the body settled, the practice of meditation moves into the realm of breath control, or pranayama. Controlling the breath is a powerful technique for calming the mind and preparing it for deeper meditation. The Gita suggests a disciplined approach to breathing, where the breath is carefully observed and regulated. This practice helps in withdrawing the senses from external objects, an essential step in achieving inward focus and reducing mental distractions.

The core of meditation as taught in the Gita is the focus on the self, or the Atman. Krishna advises practitioners to meditate with the mind and intellect dedicated solely to the self, relinquishing thoughts and attachments that cause distraction and agitation. This intense focus on the self helps in dissolving the ego, the false sense of individual identity, which is often a barrier to spiritual growth and inner peace.

Krishna emphasizes that meditation should be practiced regularly and with sincere dedication. It is not an occasional activity but a disciplined practice that requires perseverance and commitment. The regularity of meditation fortifies the mind, building its capacity to remain focused and undisturbed by the chaos of everyday life. This steadfastness is crucial for advancing in the spiritual path and for cultivating a state of continuous peace and joy.

The benefits of meditation extend beyond personal tranquility. As the meditator progresses, they experience a profound transformation in their perception of the world. The practice leads to a heightened state of awareness where one sees the interconnectedness of all life. This vision fosters a deep sense of compassion and understanding towards others, driving the meditator to act with kindness and consideration.

Furthermore, meditation deepens one's understanding of the nature of reality. It gradually reveals the illusory nature of the material world and the eternal truth of the spiritual realm. This realization liberates the practitioner from suffering and sorrow, as they come to understand that true happiness and peace are not dependent on external circumstances but are found within.

In the advanced stages of meditation, the distinction between the meditator, the act of meditation, and the object of meditation begins to dissolve. This state, known as samadhi, represents the ultimate goal of meditation—complete union with the divine. In samadhi, the individual consciousness merges with the universal consciousness, leading to an experience of bliss and oneness with all existence.

The journey of meditation, as outlined in the Bhagavad Gita, is both a science and an art. It requires technical skill in handling the mind and body, as well as an artistic touch in cultivating the subtler realms of intuition and emotion. Through this balanced approach, meditation emerges not just as a tool for relaxation or stress relief but as a profound discipline for achieving deep self-discovery, inner peace, and ultimate spiritual liberation.

ॐॐॐ

"In the clarity of wisdom, the fires of desire extinguish, and peace is kindled. The Bhagavad Gita guides us to seek knowledge not just as information but as transformative insight. With understanding comes liberation—from ignorance, from suffering, and from the cycles of compulsion."

ᐅᐅᐅ

EIGHT

UNDERSTANDING THE DIVINE

In the seventh chapter of the Bhagavad Gita, Krishna begins to unfold the profound layers of spiritual wisdom, central to which is the understanding of the divine. This chapter serves as a pivotal point where Krishna reveals insights into the nature of divinity and its integral role in human life. He explains how recognizing and connecting with a higher power not only enriches one's spiritual journey but also elevates and inspires the human spirit in everyday life.

Krishna introduces the concept of divinity by distinguishing between the material and the spiritual worlds. He explains that the universe is made up of two aspects: the lower, which consists of the earth and the elements that make up the physical world, and the higher, which is the spiritual essence that pervades and sustains all life. This higher nature is divine, eternal, and immutable, unlike the transient and changeable material nature. By understanding these two aspects, individuals can begin to comprehend the full spectrum of existence and the role of the divine within it.

At the core of Krishna's teachings in this chapter is the notion that all of creation is a manifestation of the divine. Every living being, every element in nature, and every moment of existence are imbued with divinity. However, the divine is not just an external force; it is also inherent within each individual. Recognizing this internal aspect of the divine is crucial for spiritual growth and enlightenment.

Krishna emphasizes that this realization of the divine within oneself leads to a profound transformation in how one perceives the world and interacts with it. When individuals acknowledge the divine presence within themselves, they begin to see it in others and in all aspects of the natural world. This perception fosters a sense of deep connectedness and unity with the universe, promoting feelings of love, compassion, and empathy towards others.

The process of recognizing the divine is not merely an intellectual exercise but a deeply personal and experiential journey. Krishna advises that this journey begins with faith and devotion. By cultivating a sincere devotion to the divine, individuals can develop a closer relationship with it, allowing them to receive divine grace. This grace is instrumental in lifting the veils of ignorance that cloud human understanding, thereby enabling individuals to perceive the true nature of reality.

Krishna also discusses the obstacles that prevent people from recognizing and connecting with the divine. One of the primary obstacles is attachment to material possessions and pleasures, which can distract individuals from their spiritual goals. Another significant barrier is the ego, which fosters a sense of separation and individuality that stands in contrast to the universal oneness taught in spiritual traditions.

To overcome these obstacles, Krishna recommends the practice of meditation, selfless service, and the study of sacred texts, which help cultivate a higher awareness and reduce attachments and ego. These practices enable individuals to purify their hearts and minds, making them receptive to the subtleties of spiritual truths.

Furthermore, understanding the divine involves recognizing its omnipotence and omniscience. Krishna describes how all qualities and phenomena in the world, whether perceived as positive or negative, are manifestations of the divine. This realization helps individuals transcend dualistic thinking and embrace a more holistic view of existence where every aspect of life is seen as part of a divine play.

This holistic perspective instills a sense of peace and contentment, as individuals learn to accept life's ups and downs with equanimity. They understand that every experience, whether joyous or challenging, is an opportunity for growth and deeper understanding. This acceptance is crucial for maintaining inner peace and for navigating the complexities of life with grace and wisdom.

In summary, the teachings of the Gita in this chapter not only deepen one's understanding of the divine but also illustrate how this understanding can transform one's life. Recognizing and connecting with the divine inspires a profound shift in perspective—from a self-centered view of existence to a more expansive, inclusive, and compassionate outlook. This shift is not only uplifting for the individual but also beneficial for society at large, as it promotes values of unity, peace, and universal love. Thus, the journey to understanding the divine is both a personal quest for spiritual enlightenment and a transformative pathway that can lead to a more harmonious and fulfilling life.

ॐॐॐ

"Renunciation is not about forsaking the world but about embracing life fully without attachment to the fleeting. By understanding the impermanence of material gains, as taught in the Gita, we learn to cherish what truly matters—relationships, integrity, and the growth of the soul."

▷▷▷

NINE

THE ETERNAL SPIRIT

The eighth chapter of the Bhagavad Gita presents profound insights into the immortal nature of the soul, exploring its journey beyond the confines of physical existence. This exploration not only deepens the understanding of what it means to be truly alive but also provides a compass for navigating the transient world with a sense of eternal purpose.

At the heart of this chapter is the teaching that the soul, or Atman, is eternal and indestructible. Unlike the physical body, which is subject to decay and death, the soul never perishes; it transcends the cycle of birth and death. Krishna emphasizes that this understanding is crucial for anyone seeking spiritual enlightenment and liberation. He explains that the physical world, including our bodies and the material environment, is temporary and constantly changing, whereas the soul remains constant and unchanging. This distinction helps in cultivating detachment from the material aspects of life and focusing on the spiritual growth that defines the essence of one's true self.

Krishna delves into the mechanics of the soul's journey after physical death, explaining the various paths that souls may take. These paths are determined by an individual's actions, thoughts, and desires at the time of death. He distinguishes between two primary paths: the path of the sun, which leads to liberation and is taken by those who are aware of the self and devoted to spiritual practices; and the path of the moon, which leads to rebirth and is taken by those who are still attached to the pleasures and desires of the material world. These paths symbolize the dual outcomes based on one's life choices and spiritual preparedness.

To navigate towards the path of the sun, Krishna advises constant meditation on the divine, particularly at the time of death. The last thoughts and consciousness at the time of death have a significant impact on the soul's destiny. Therefore, he encourages practicing mindfulness and remembrance of the divine throughout one's life, so that these practices become second nature and prevail at the moment of death. This teaching underscores the importance of a disciplined spiritual life where every action, thought, and meditation is aligned with the higher goal of attaining oneness with the divine.

Krishna also introduces the concept of Brahman, the ultimate, unmanifested reality that encompasses everything. He explains that understanding the nature of Brahman is essential for realizing the soul's eternal aspect. Brahman is beyond birth and death, and it is the final destination for the soul that escapes the cycle of rebirth. This realization offers a profound comfort and a sense of peace, knowing that the trials and tribulations of life are but brief episodes in the grand continuum of existence.

The journey of the soul is not merely about transcending the physical realm but also about understanding the lessons each life experience offers. Life's experiences are designed to teach specific lessons necessary for the soul's evolution towards greater awareness and spiritual maturity. Thus, understanding the eternal nature of the soul helps individuals to view life as a series of opportunities for growth and learning, rather than a sequence of random, meaningless events.

Furthermore, the Gita explains that the actions performed in one's life significantly impact the soul's journey. Actions imbued with selflessness, compassion, and a spirit of service purify the soul, making it suitable for higher spiritual realms. Conversely, actions driven by selfishness, greed, and ignorance bind the soul to the material world, leading to rebirth and continued suffering. This karmic principle emphasizes the role of free will and ethical living in shaping the soul's trajectory.

Krishna's teachings about the eternal spirit are not only intended to provide knowledge but also to inspire a shift in perspective—from a focus on temporary material gains to long-term spiritual values. This shift has profound implications for how individuals live their daily lives. It encourages values such as integrity, humility, and kindness, knowing that these qualities resonate with the soul's eternal nature and its divine journey.

In essence, the understanding of the soul's eternal nature and its journey beyond physical existence opens up new dimensions of meaning in life. It provides a framework within which the ephemeral nature of human experiences can be navigated with wisdom and equanimity. This perspective nurtures a deep sense of inner peace and fulfillment, as individuals align their earthly journey with the soul's divine nature, embracing the transient world while keeping their sights on the eternal. Thus, the teachings of the Gita serve as a guide for living a life that is both grounded in reality and elevated by the knowledge of the immortal spirit, crafting a path that leads to ultimate liberation and unity with the divine.

ॐॐॐ

"Faith in the Gita is not blind adherence but a luminous path to the divine, lit by the lamp of knowledge. Trust the wisdom of the ages; let it guide your steps in the dance of life. Where faith leads, courage and clarity follow."

🖤🖤🖤

TEN

The Royal Knowledge and the Royal Secret

The ninth chapter of the Bhagavad Gita is a pivotal point where Krishna imparts to Arjuna what he describes as the most profound spiritual knowledge and secrets. This knowledge, deemed royal because of its supreme and sovereign nature, illuminates the mysteries that govern life and the universe. It is a knowledge that not only enlightens but also liberates, offering a clear path to understanding and ultimate liberation.

Krishna begins by emphasizing the sacred and confidential nature of this wisdom. He describes it as the king of sciences, the most secret, pure, and supreme knowledge and realization. It is accessible to those who possess devotion and is directly realizable, practical, and eternal.

The knowledge revealed in this chapter deals with the nature of the universe, the role of the divine within it, and the interplay between the temporal and the eternal, the manifest and the unmanifest.

Central to this chapter is the concept of divine omnipresence. Krishna reveals that although he is beyond the physical manifestations and is not visible to the ordinary eye, he is the underlying essence of all that exists. He is both immanent and transcendent, pervading the entire universe yet separate from it. This duality is one of the profound mysteries of the spiritual path—understanding how the divine can be both within everything and yet beyond all.

Krishna explains that all beings in the universe, from the smallest to the greatest, are manifestations of his energy. He is the source of all creation and the ultimate cause of all causes. Yet, despite his omnipresence, he remains detached and unaffected by his creations.

This concept of divine detachment is another royal secret, teaching that true power lies in the ability to remain unaffected by the dualities of the world such as birth and death, joy and sorrow, success and failure.

The mystery deepens as Krishna discusses how he sustains and governs the cosmos with a mere fraction of his energy. This highlights the infinite power and glory of the divine, which orchestrates the vast and complex mechanisms of the universe without any strain. Understanding this aspect of the divine encourages a profound respect and awe for the majesty of creation and the creator.

Krishna also reveals the impact of divine energy on human action. He discusses how, despite the appearance of free will, all actions are influenced by nature's qualities (gunas) which, in turn, are controlled by divine energy.

This revelation shifts the perception of personal agency, urging an understanding of life as a play of cosmic energies where one's alignment with these energies determines their path and progress.

The divine promise of liberation is another significant aspect of the royal knowledge. Krishna assures that those who understand and embrace this knowledge are not bound by their actions but are liberated from the cycle of birth and death. This liberation is not just from physical existence but from the ignorance and limitations that bind the soul.

The path to this understanding and liberation is through unwavering faith and devotion. Krishna emphasizes that devotion to the divine is the most potent means to assimilate this profound knowledge. Devotion purifies the heart and mind, enabling the devotee to perceive and experience the divine presence in all aspects of life.

Krishna then explains the universal applicability of this knowledge, stating that it transcends all barriers of caste, creed, and social status. Anyone who sincerely seeks this knowledge and approaches the divine with devotion can attain it, irrespective of their background or past actions.

This inclusivity is a fundamental principle of the royal knowledge, making it a universal path to enlightenment and liberation.

Furthermore, the practical application of this royal knowledge involves seeing the divine in every aspect of creation and recognizing that all actions should be performed as offerings to the divine. This shift in perception transforms ordinary life into a spiritual practice, where every action becomes an act of worship and a step towards liberation.

The royal knowledge and the royal secret revealed in this chapter of the Bhagavad Gita offer a profound understanding of life and the universe. They provide insights into the nature of the divine, the structure of the cosmos, and the path to liberation.

By embracing these truths, one can live a life of greater awareness, purpose, and freedom, aligned with the cosmic order and enriched by the eternal presence of the divine. This knowledge is not just philosophical but intensely practical, offering guidance for living a life that is deeply connected to the spiritual essence of existence.

"The Gita does not call us to withdraw from the world but to engage with it more consciously and wholeheartedly. It teaches that every action, grounded in righteousness, has the power to shape destinies. Act with purpose, act with love, and let every deed sing a song of dharma."

ᕕᕕᕕ

ELEVEN

MANIFESTING THE DIVINE

The tenth chapter of the Bhagavad Gita offers profound insights into recognizing and appreciating the divine qualities that permeate both the world around us and the inner realm of our own beings. This chapter is a beautiful exposition on the manifestations of the divine, providing practical guidance for identifying and embracing these aspects in everyday life.

Krishna, speaking to Arjuna, reveals how the divine essence infuses the universe, illustrating this through the enumeration of his divine manifestations. He identifies himself with the highest and most powerful qualities found in nature, human beings, and the cosmic order. For instance, Krishna describes himself as the strength of the strong, devoid of passion and desire, the intelligence of the intelligent, the splendor of the splendid, and the essence in every heart.

This description serves as a guide for recognizing the divine qualities that are present in all aspects of creation. The recognition of these qualities involves seeing beyond the ordinary and perceiving the extraordinary that lies within the mundane. It is about understanding that every form of excellence, every instance of beauty, and every manifestation of strength and virtue originates from the divine.

Krishna further emphasizes that these manifestations are not just high concepts but are tangible and can be observed daily. For instance, the brilliance of the sun that lights up the sky, the grandeur of the moon that illuminates the night, the vastness of the ocean, and the majesty of the mountains are all reflections of divine qualities. In humans, attributes such as intelligence, courage, strength, and compassion are considered divine because they elevate human nature and lead to greater good.

Appreciating these divine qualities requires a shift in perception. It entails developing an awareness that every good quality, every act of kindness, and every truth is a manifestation of the divine. This realization helps in cultivating a sense of connectedness with the larger cosmos and inspires an attitude of reverence and gratitude towards life and its myriad expressions.

The process of recognizing and appreciating the divine also involves introspection and self-awareness. Krishna points out that the divine resides in the heart of every being. This inner divinity is the source of all inspiration, creativity, and wisdom. By turning inward through meditation and contemplative practices, one can tap into this internal reservoir of divinity. This self-realization empowers individuals to transcend their limitations and align their actions with higher principles.

Moreover, Krishna discusses how the divine qualities can be actively cultivated through devotion and righteous living. By engaging in practices that enhance one's spiritual qualities—such as honesty, non-violence, compassion, and self-control—one not only honors the divine within oneself but also contributes to the upliftment of society. Each act of virtue is seen as an offering to the divine, an expression of the divine qualities that one seeks to embody.

Cultivating an appreciation for the divine also means recognizing the divine in others. This involves respecting the dignity of all beings and acknowledging that everyone, regardless of their background or circumstances, embodies aspects of the divine. This recognition can profoundly change interpersonal relationships, fostering a more compassionate, understanding, and harmonious interaction between individuals.

The chapter also stresses the joy and fulfillment that come from living in harmony with the divine qualities. Krishna explains that those who recognize and celebrate the divine in their lives are bestowed with profound peace and spiritual abundance. They are guided by divine wisdom in their decisions and actions, which leads to a life of purpose and satisfaction.

In sum, the teaching of manifesting the divine in the tenth chapter of the Bhagavad Gita offers both a vision and a practical pathway for spiritual growth. It encourages us to look within and around, to recognize the divine qualities that manifest in various forms, and to appreciate and cultivate these qualities in our lives. By doing so, we not only enhance our own spiritual well-being but also contribute to the creation of a more just, compassionate, and enlightened world. This approach transforms ordinary living into a divine journey, filled with purpose, grace, and an enduring connection to the universal spirit.

꘍꘍꘍

"Balance in thought, word, and deed is the essence
of a life well-lived, a central teaching of the Gita.
Strive not for perfection but for harmony within
and without. In balance, find the rhythm that
dances to the timeless tune of ethical living."

ᚦᚦᚦ

TWELVE

THE VISION OF THE UNIVERSAL FORM

The eleventh chapter of the Bhagavad Gita presents one of the most majestic and awe-inspiring revelations—the universal form of Krishna, which symbolizes the vastness of the universe and the intricate interconnectedness of all life. This vision granted to Arjuna serves as a profound spiritual lesson on the omnipresence of the divine and the unity underlying the apparent diversity in the world.

As Arjuna stands on the battlefield, prepared to engage in a war that pits him against his own kin, he is granted the divine eyesight necessary to perceive Krishna's universal form. This form is not just a figure but an encompassing presence that spans the entirety of creation, embodying all gods, creatures, and the entire cosmos within its being. Arjuna sees in Krishna's body the entire universe, drawn together into one infinite, divine entity that transcends time and space.

This vision is overwhelming; it encompasses the beautiful and the terrifying, the minuscule and the infinite. Arjuna sees creation and destruction happening simultaneously—fires that consume worlds, faces beaming with divine light, and mouths that devour all beings.

He sees the past, present, and future all at once, without the constraints of time as humans understand it. This direct perception of Krishna's cosmic form reveals the ultimate reality that underlies all appearances and the interconnectedness of all forms of life.

The vision of the universal form also teaches the profound lesson that every individual life, every event in the history of the universe, is interconnected in an intricate web of causality and influence. Each action, each life, no matter how significant or insignificant it appears, plays a role in the divine cosmic play. This understanding can profoundly shift how one views their actions and their consequences on the environment and on other beings.

This interconnectedness implies a shared destiny and a collective responsibility towards the well-being of all. It suggests that the separation between individuals is an illusion; at a fundamental level, everyone and everything is part of the same divine essence. This realization fosters a sense of empathy and unity, urging individuals to act with consideration and compassion towards others and the natural world.

Furthermore, the vision of the universal form highlights the importance of humility in the face of the divine and the vast mysteries of the universe. Arjuna, witnessing this form, feels both terror and awe but also a deep reverence and devotion. He realizes the limits of his own understanding and the boundless nature of the divine. This humility is a crucial virtue for anyone on a spiritual path, as it opens the heart to deeper knowledge and wisdom.

The teaching about the universal form of Krishna also addresses the nature of reality itself. It suggests that while the physical world may appear diverse and full of contradictions, there is an underlying unity that holds everything together. This unity is the divine essence, which manifests itself in myriad forms and phenomena. By meditating on this unity, one can transcend the superficial differences and conflicts that often divide humanity.

Moreover, the vision of the universal form underscores the idea of divine omnipotence and omniscience. It conveys that nothing is beyond the divine's influence or understanding. This assurance can be a source of great comfort and strength, particularly in times of confusion and despair. It encourages a trust in the divine order of things, even when the world seems chaotic and unpredictable.

In practical terms, reflecting on the vastness of the universe and the interconnectedness of all life can lead to a more holistic and integrated approach to living. It encourages sustainability, ethical behavior, and a proactive engagement in making the world a better place. Recognizing the divine in every aspect of the world enhances one's ability to live a life that is not only personally fulfilling but also beneficial to the broader community and the world.

In essence, the eleventh chapter of the Gita invites one to embrace a broader perspective of existence, one that acknowledges and reveres the interconnectedness and sacredness of all life. This perspective is essential for cultivating a deep-seated peace and a purposeful existence, rooted in the understanding of life's divine unity and the responsibilities it entails. Through this understanding, one can truly begin to appreciate the beauty and complexity of the cosmos and their place within it, leading to a life lived with greater awareness, compassion, and harmony.

ॐॐॐ

"Let your life be a reflection of the beauty and depth of your soul. The Gita teaches us that the outer world is a mirror of the inner. Cultivate inner beauty, and it will manifest in your actions and your interactions."

ᐅᐅᐅ

THIRTEEN

THE PATH OF DEVOTION

The twelfth chapter of the Bhagavad Gita introduces Bhakti Yoga, the path of devotion, which emphasizes cultivating love, trust, and devotion not only towards the divine but as a fundamental approach to all relationships and life itself. This chapter beautifully outlines how the practice of Bhakti Yoga can transform personal connections and foster a deep sense of unity and purpose in the practitioner's life.

Bhakti Yoga is described as the process of deepening one's devotion towards the divine, seeing and serving the divine in all beings. It involves channeling all emotions, actions, and thoughts towards God, transforming mundane experiences into spiritual offerings. This path is accessible to anyone, regardless of their social status, background, or intellectual capacity, making it a profoundly democratic spiritual practice.

The essence of Bhakti Yoga lies in its simplicity and the purity of heart it cultivates. Krishna explains that what matters most on this path is not ritualistic practices or scholarly knowledge but a sincere, unwavering devotion to the divine. This devotion is characterized by love and trust and is manifest through a variety of practices such as chanting, meditation, prayer, and service to others, all of which are expressions of love towards God.

Krishna assures Arjuna that those who set their hearts on him, worship him with unfaltering faith, and dedicate every action to him, are held in high esteem. This reassurance highlights the importance of faith and the emotional bond between the devotee and the divine, suggesting that the strength of this bond can overcome any obstacle in the path of spiritual progress.

The practice of Bhakti Yoga also extends beyond individual spirituality to influence one's relationships with others. By viewing others as manifestations of the divine, practitioners of Bhakti learn to approach relationships with the same love, reverence, and devotion that they offer to God. This perspective transforms interactions, promoting a more compassionate, empathetic, and forgiving attitude. In family life, work, or community interactions, the devotee seeks to serve others selflessly, recognizing that such service is also service to the divine.

Moreover, Bhakti Yoga fosters trust in the divine plan, helping individuals to overcome anxiety and uncertainty about the future. This trust is cultivated through the understanding that everything is under the divine's control and that each life is guided by a higher wisdom. Such faith provides a profound sense of security and peace, allowing devotees to handle life's challenges with greater equanimity and resilience.

The cultivation of love in Bhakti Yoga is not passive but an active and dynamic force that propels individuals to engage deeply with life. Love, in the context of Bhakti Yoga, involves seeing the world through the eyes of affection and unity, seeking to contribute positively and create harmony. This active love is transformative, capable of dissolving barriers of hatred, prejudice, and isolation.

Krishna emphasizes that the path of devotion is the quickest and most effective means to achieve divine consciousness and liberation. This is because devotion directly purifies the heart and aligns the human will with divine will, leading to an accelerated spiritual growth. Devotees on this path experience a gradual expansion of consciousness, beginning to perceive the divine presence in all things and becoming more attuned to spiritual realities.

The teachings on Bhakti Yoga also address the qualities that make a devotee dear to the divine. These include non-envy, kindness, forgiveness, contentment, purity, and self-control, among others. Cultivating these qualities ensures that the devotee's heart is prepared to receive and retain divine love, further deepening their spiritual journey.

The path of Bhakti Yoga as outlined in the Bhagavad Gita offers a profound spiritual practice that enriches not only the individual's inner life but also their external interactions. By fostering love, trust, and devotion, Bhakti Yoga transforms the nature of relationships, turning everyday encounters into spiritual exchanges. This path not only promises ultimate liberation but also enhances the quality of daily life, filling it with love, peace, and a deep sense of divine connection. Through Bhakti Yoga, the ordinary becomes infused with the extraordinary, revealing the sacred in the simplest moments of life.

ppp

"Detachment is not disengagement but the highest
form of passionate living. According to the Gita, by
detaching from outcomes, we engage with life on a
deeper level, experiencing the fullness of each
moment. Live passionately, love freely, and act
fearlessly."

ᐅᐅᐅ

FOURTEEN

THE FIELD AND THE KNOWER OF THE FIELD

The thirteenth chapter of the Bhagavad Gita introduces a profound and illuminating discourse on the nature of reality through the metaphors of the "field" (Kshetra) and the "knower of the field" (Kshetrajna). This analogy serves to deepen the understanding of the relationship between the body and the soul, and underscores the importance of self-awareness and responsibility in the journey toward spiritual enlightenment.

The "field" represents the body along with the physical world and all perceivable phenomena, including the senses, material elements, mind, and emotions. Essentially, it encompasses all that is subject to change, decay, and death—everything that is objectively observable and interactable in the physical realm. In contrast, the "knower of the field" symbolizes the soul, or consciousness, which observes and experiences the field but remains distinct and unaltered by it. This knower is the true self, the essence of being that is eternal, unchanging, and indivisible.

Krishna emphasizes that understanding the distinction between the field and the knower of the field is critical for spiritual knowledge. This understanding leads to a realization of one's true nature as not merely the body or the mind but as the observing consciousness. Such realization is the foundation of self-awareness, where an individual becomes a witness to their own life, observing thoughts, emotions, and sensations without identifying with them.

The relationship between the field and the knower of the field is central to the concept of responsibility. When one identifies with the body (the field), they become entangled in the material world, leading to actions driven by desire, fear, and attachment, which further bind the soul to the cycle of birth and death. However, by recognizing themselves as the knower of the field, individuals can rise above these bindings. They start acting from a place of consciousness and choice rather than from compulsion driven by the egoistic self.

This shift in identification fosters a profound sense of responsibility. It is no longer just about personal success or survival, but about how one's actions affect their spiritual growth and the world around them. This sense of responsibility is deeply empowering because it is aligned with the soul's nature, which is inherently free, peaceful, and compassionate.

Self-awareness cultivated through understanding the knower of the field enables individuals to witness their own mental and emotional patterns without being swept away by them. This awareness creates a space of inner freedom where one can choose responses rather than reacting impulsively. This choice is the exercise of true freedom and the basis of ethical living. It allows individuals to live in harmony with their higher selves and universal laws, leading to actions that are beneficial not only to oneself but also to others.

Moreover, the recognition of the knower of the field encourages a deeper exploration of life's purpose and meaning. It raises fundamental questions about the origin, nature, and destiny of consciousness, prompting individuals to seek knowledge beyond the material and transient. This quest for deeper understanding elevates the human experience, providing a broader context in which life's challenges and experiences can be interpreted.

Krishna also elaborates on the qualities necessary to perceive the distinction between the field and the knower effectively. These include humility, sincerity, non-violence, patience, integrity, self-restraint, dispassion towards the objects of the senses, and absence of ego. Cultivating these qualities not only purifies the mind but also sharpens one's perception, allowing for a clearer understanding of the spiritual truths.

In practical terms, the knowledge of the field and the knower of the field has significant implications for daily living. It encourages a life of mindfulness, where every moment is an opportunity to practice awareness and self-reflection. This mindful living leads to a more conscious existence, where choices are made with consideration of their higher impact and alignment with one's true nature.

The discourse on the field and the knower of the field in the Bhagavad Gita offers a comprehensive framework for understanding the human condition and the path to liberation. By distinguishing between the temporal physical existence and the eternal spiritual essence, it provides a guide for living a life of heightened awareness and responsibility. This understanding not only enriches one's spiritual journey but also enhances the quality of everyday life, making it a purposeful and enlightened experience.

ॐॐॐ

"In the silence of meditation, the Gita whispers truths of the cosmos. Listen intently, for in these moments of stillness, wisdom unfolds. Meditation is the journey inward that leads to an expansive outward life."

▷▷▷

FIFTEEN

The Forces of Evolution

The fourteenth chapter of the Bhagavad Gita delves deeply into the concept of the three gunas or qualities—sattva, rajas, and tamas—that are said to be the forces of evolution and the fundamental elements influencing human character and behavior. This intricate teaching explores how these qualities manifest within individuals, shaping their actions, reactions, desires, and ultimately their spiritual progress.

The gunas are described as the primal forces that constitute the material universe, including the human psyche. Each person, object, and experience is a combination of these three gunas, but the proportion and dominance of one guna over the others determine the nature of the entity or experience. Understanding these gunas provides insight into the dynamics of human behavior and offers a framework for personal and spiritual development.

Sattva is the quality of goodness, harmony, and balance. It is characterized by purity, wisdom, and tranquility. Individuals in whom sattva predominates display qualities such as compassion, mindfulness, and a deep-seated peace. They are drawn to activities that promote harmony and constructive growth, both for themselves and for others. Sattva enhances clarity of mind and promotes contentment and joy. However, when sattva becomes excessive or attached, it can lead to attachment to knowledge, comfort, and a subtle sense of pride or superiority.

Rajas represents the quality of passion, activity, and restlessness. It is associated with desire, thirst for life, and attachment to outcomes. Rajasic individuals are highly dynamic, ambitious, and energetic, driven by a strong desire to achieve and conquer. This quality fuels progress and change but can also lead to dissatisfaction, agitation, and conflict, as it binds the soul to action and desire. Excessive rajas is marked by a constant state of unrest and a pervasive sense of never being satisfied, pushing individuals toward endless activity without peace.

Tamas is the quality of darkness, inertia, and ignorance. It manifests as laziness, confusion, and delusion. When tamas dominates, it hampers perception and dulls the senses, leading to a lack of motivation and understanding, incorrect understanding, and an inability to see things as they are. Tamasic behavior includes tendencies toward destruction, deceit, and irresponsibility. This quality is a significant barrier to spiritual enlightenment as it fosters ignorance and disconnection from the true nature of self and reality.

The Bhagavad Gita explains that these gunas exist in dynamic interplay and their balance can shift throughout one's life due to various influences, including diet, lifestyle, and mental activities. For instance, certain foods can increase one quality over others; fresh, wholesome foods enhance sattva, overly spicy or rich foods stir rajas, and stale or impure substances strengthen tamas.

To advance spiritually, the Gita advises cultivating sattva while reducing the influence of rajas and tamas. This is achieved through disciplined practices including meditation, proper diet, ethical living, and the pursuit of knowledge. Cultivating sattva enhances one's capacity for self-reflection, which is essential for recognizing the influences of all three gunas in one's thoughts, decisions, and actions.

Understanding and managing the gunas is crucial for anyone on a spiritual path, as it directly impacts one's ability to attain higher states of consciousness. A sattvic state is most conducive to achieving self-realization because it supports a clear, calm, and focused mind, which is necessary for deep meditation and spiritual insight. However, the ultimate goal is to transcend all three gunas, reaching a state of pure transcendence where one is not influenced by any of the material qualities. This state of transcendence is described as beyond darkness, beyond the effects of material actions, and beyond dualities.

In practical terms, applying the knowledge of the gunas involves observing one's own nature and behaviors to understand which guna is predominant at any given time and making conscious choices to cultivate more sattva. This awareness allows individuals to steer their actions and thoughts toward greater harmony and spiritual alignment.

In summary, the discussion of the gunas in the Bhagavad Gita provides a profound framework for understanding human psychology and behavior from a spiritual perspective. By recognizing the influences of sattva, rajas, and tamas, individuals can work towards balancing these forces within themselves, leading to enhanced self-awareness, better control over their actions and reactions, and ultimately, progress on their spiritual journey. This journey involves not only living a life of ethical and spiritual integrity but also striving towards transcendence, where one is no longer bound by the fluctuations of the gunas, free to experience the ultimate reality that lies beyond.

ၯၯၯ

"Compassion is the true communication of souls, a
lesson brightly illuminated in the Gita. See yourself
in others, understand their joys and their struggles.
In this shared understanding, kindness flows
naturally."

♡♡♡

SIXTEEN

THE SUPREME SELF

The fifteenth chapter of the Bhagavad Gita presents a profound exploration of the concept of the Supreme Self, elucidating how understanding this fundamental aspect of existence can lead individuals to realize their highest potential. This chapter offers both a philosophical foundation and a practical approach to spiritual growth, emphasizing the eternal nature of the soul and its intrinsic connection with the divine.

The Supreme Self, or Purushottama, is described as the ultimate reality that transcends the temporal and the ephemeral aspects of the world. It is both immanent, existing within every living being, and transcendent, surpassing the limitations of the material universe. This dual nature of the Supreme Self makes it the essence of all that exists and the source of all life.

Understanding the Supreme Self begins with the recognition that our individual self, or atman, is not separate from the cosmic spirit, or Brahman. The individual self is essentially a reflection of the Supreme Self, similar to how the sun reflects on countless bodies of water. Though appearing as many, the sun remains one. Similarly, the Supreme Self, the ultimate source of consciousness, illuminates every living being, giving life and purpose to the universe.

This realization is crucial in unlocking one's highest potential because it shifts the focus from the transient to the eternal. Often, human endeavors are directed towards achieving success, pleasure, or security within the material realm, but these pursuits can lead to a cycle of dissatisfaction and perpetual striving. By recognizing the Supreme Self as the true goal of life, individuals can transcend these limited aspirations and engage in actions that foster spiritual growth and enlightenment.

The Gita metaphorically describes the material world as an upside-down tree, with its roots upwards and branches down. This tree represents the material reality, which is subject to change, decay, and death. However, the roots, symbolizing the Supreme Self, are eternal and unchanging. Understanding this analogy encourages individuals to strive upwards, towards the roots, seeking a deeper, spiritual understanding of existence rather than becoming entangled in the impermanent aspects of life.

The journey towards realizing the Supreme Self involves detaching from the material aspects of the world and nurturing qualities that align with spiritual principles. This process is facilitated by practices such as meditation, devotion, self-discipline, and selfless service. These practices help purify the mind and heart, enabling individuals to experience their true nature as part of the divine.

Moreover, the Gita emphasizes that realizing the Supreme Self leads to liberation (moksha). Liberation in this context means freedom from the cycle of birth and death (samsara) and the accompanying suffering. It is achieved when an individual fully understands and experiences their oneness with the Supreme Self, leading to the dissolution of ego and individuality. This state of being is characterized by perpetual peace, boundless joy, and unshakeable contentment.

The relevance of the Supreme Self in daily life is also profound. By anchoring one's identity in the eternal aspect of the self rather than the temporal, one's perspective on life radically changes. Challenges and hardships are viewed as opportunities for growth, interactions are infused with compassion and empathy, and successes and failures are met with equanimity. This shift in perspective fosters a life of harmony, balance, and purpose, aligning one's actions with higher spiritual values.

Additionally, understanding the Supreme Self cultivates a sense of universal responsibility. Recognizing the divine in oneself and others promotes respect for all life and encourages actions that contribute to the welfare of the community and the environment. This sense of connectedness with all of existence is a powerful motivator for ethical behavior and selfless action.

The concept of the Supreme Self as presented in the Bhagavad Gita offers a transformative perspective on human existence. It encourages individuals to look beyond the superficial and transient pleasures of the world and to seek fulfillment in the eternal and unchanging reality of the Supreme Self. By aligning oneself with this ultimate reality, one can discover and realize their highest potential, leading a life of deep satisfaction, purpose, and spiritual liberation. This journey not only enhances one's own life but also has the potential to elevate the lives of others, creating a more compassionate and enlightened world.

ᐁᐁᐁ

"Every act of learning is an act of spiritual growth, echoing the teachings of the Gita. Embrace knowledge not just to inform but to transform. Let learning be an act of devotion, bringing you closer to your highest self."

❥❥❥

SEVENTEEN

DISTINGUISHING THE DIVINE AND THE DEMONIC

The sixteenth chapter of the Bhagavad Gita provides a clear distinction between what are termed as divine and demonic qualities. This discourse serves as a critical guide for individuals striving to foster their inherent divine nature while curbing and transforming the negative, destructive tendencies that can lead to suffering and spiritual degradation. Understanding and applying these teachings is crucial for personal growth and spiritual evolution.

The Gita describes divine qualities as those that foster harmony, truth, and spiritual progress. These include fearlessness, purity of heart, self-control, sacrifice, study of sacred texts, austerity, straightforwardness, non-violence, truthfulness, freedom from anger, renunciation, tranquility, aversion to fault-finding, compassion towards all beings, absence of greed, gentleness, modesty, and steady determination. These qualities are not just ethical guidelines but are deeply integrated into the very fabric of spiritual consciousness. They are inherent in the soul's pure state and are reflective of one's higher self, which is eternally connected with the divine.

Cultivating these divine qualities requires consistent practice and sincere commitment. It involves daily self-reflection to recognize one's weaknesses and strengths, continuous learning through sacred texts and teachings, and the regular practice of spiritual disciplines like meditation, prayer, and service. Moreover, associating with spiritually inclined individuals and communities can significantly bolster one's efforts in cultivating these qualities. Such environments provide support, inspiration, and practical guidance, making the path towards spiritual maturity more accessible and engaging.

Conversely, the Gita talks about demonic qualities which lead to bondage and suffering. These include hypocrisy, arrogance, self-conceit, anger, harshness, and ignorance. These traits arise from a fundamental misunderstanding of one's true nature and purpose in life. Instead of recognizing their inherent divinity and interconnectedness with all of existence, individuals with these tendencies see themselves as separate, leading to selfish actions and desires that disregard the well-being of others and the moral laws of the universe.

Overcoming these negative tendencies involves a deep and often challenging process of inner transformation. This transformation can be facilitated through the practice of mindfulness, which helps bring awareness to one's thoughts, emotions, and behaviors, allowing for greater self-control and the ability to make conscious choices. Additionally, engaging in selfless service can shift one's focus from self-centered motivations to actions that benefit others, fostering a sense of empathy and connection.

The Gita emphasizes the importance of self-awareness in distinguishing between these qualities. It is through self-awareness that individuals can observe their inclinations without judgment, understand their origins, and consciously choose actions that align with divine qualities. This awareness is not superficial but penetrative, reaching into the depths of one's being to effect genuine change.

Spiritual teachings and disciplines are indispensable in this endeavor. They provide the knowledge and tools needed to transform one's character from being dominated by demonic qualities to being enriched with divine qualities. This transformation is not merely about repressing negative impulses but about understanding and resolving the deeper insecurities and misconceptions that give rise to them.

Moreover, the journey from demonic to divine qualities is marked by significant inner and outer changes. Internally, one experiences a growing sense of peace, stability, and contentment. Externally, relationships become more harmonious, and actions more aligned with universal welfare. This shift greatly enhances the quality of life, not just for the individual but for all those around them.

The teachings of the Gita also underscore the consequences of allowing demonic qualities to prevail. It warns of the degradation of the soul and the inevitable pain and suffering that follow such a path. In stark contrast, cultivating divine qualities leads to liberation—freedom from the cycle of birth and death and all the suffering associated with it.

Distinguishing and cultivating divine qualities while overcoming demonic tendencies as outlined in the Bhagavad Gita is essential for anyone seeking a meaningful, fulfilled, and spiritually oriented life. This process requires vigilance, dedication, and a heartfelt desire to align with one's highest self. By embracing the divine qualities, individuals not only enhance their own lives but also contribute positively to the world, fostering a collective environment of peace, understanding, and spiritual wisdom. This transformative journey is not just about personal enlightenment but about contributing to the greater good, embodying the principles that sustain the harmony and balance of the universe.

ᏋᏋᏋ

"In humility, find the strength that pride can never bestow. The Gita teaches us that modesty is not weakness but a clear recognition of our limitations and potential. From this truth, the soul draws its power to grow and flourish."

❦❦❦

EIGHTEEN

THE POWER OF FAITH

The seventeenth chapter of the Bhagavad Gita delves into the profound influence of faith on an individual's life, articulating how it molds one's practices, decisions, and ultimately shapes destiny. Faith, as described in the Gita, is a deep-seated belief and trust that pervades a person's entire being, influencing their thoughts, actions, and their interaction with the world.

Faith in the Gita is not merely religious or spiritual belief; it encompasses all the convictions that drive an individual's daily behaviors and choices. This includes faith in certain values, ideologies, or systems of thought that determine the nature of one's actions and their ethical framework. Essentially, faith acts as the foundation upon which individuals build their lives and through which they filter their experiences and decisions.

Krishna explains that every person is inherently endowed with faith, and the nature of this faith corresponds directly to their inherent disposition, which is influenced by the three gunas—sattva, rajas, and tamas. These modes of nature not only determine physical traits but also shape the type of faith an individual gravitates towards. Sattvic faith leads to purity, wisdom, and harmony; rajasic faith engenders passion, desire, and action; tamasic faith results in ignorance, inertia, and confusion. Thus, the quality of one's faith can elevate or degrade their life path, influencing their ultimate destiny.

The impact of faith on daily practices is immense. For example, individuals with sattvic faith are drawn to practices that promote peace, cleanliness, stability, and compassion. Their rituals and routines are likely to be disciplined and reflective, fostering spiritual growth and personal well-being. On the other hand, those with rajasic faith may engage in practices that are intense, driven by success and recognition, often leading to stress and aggressive competition. Individuals with tamasic faith might neglect self-care and engage in self-destructive habits, driven by ignorance and delusion.

These practices, informed by the underlying quality of faith, deeply influence decision-making processes. Sattvic faith encourages decisions that consider long-term welfare, ethical implications, and collective harmony. Rajasic faith often results in choices that prioritize personal gain and immediate satisfaction, sometimes at the expense of others' well-being. Tamasic faith may lead to poor decision-making due to a lack of clarity and understanding, resulting in actions that are harmful or futile.

The Bhagavad Gita strongly emphasizes that one's faith can evolve and be cultivated in a direction that promotes higher virtues and greater self-awareness. This transformation is crucial as faith determines not only mundane choices but also one's spiritual trajectory. The cultivation of sattvic faith, in particular, is advocated because it leads to liberation and enlightenment—ultimate goals in Hindu spiritual practice.

Moreover, Krishna discusses the influence of faith on one's dietary habits, illustrating a direct connection between what one consumes and the nature of one's faith. Food that is pure, nourishing, and wholesome increases vitality and clarity, fostering sattvic qualities. Foods that are overly spicy, bitter, or salty stir passion and restlessness, reflecting rajasic qualities, while stale, impure, and overcooked foods contribute to lethargy and ignorance, characteristic of tamasic qualities.

The discussion extends beyond mere food to include all forms of consumption, including the information and sensory experiences one absorbs. This holistic approach shows that faith deeply impacts one's physical, mental, and spiritual health, underscoring the necessity of mindful consumption in maintaining a healthy and balanced life.

Faith also plays a pivotal role in enduring adversity. With strong faith, individuals find the strength to face challenges and overcome obstacles. It provides a reservoir of courage and perseverance, enabling individuals to pursue their goals despite difficulties. This resilience, fueled by faith, is often what distinguishes those who achieve their life's purposes from those who falter.

In sum, the seventeenth chapter of the Bhagavad Gita reveals the transformative power of faith in shaping an individual's life. It shows how faith molds one's personality, influences choices, dictates practices, and ultimately directs destiny. By understanding and cultivating a higher quality of faith, individuals can align their lives with their highest ideals and aspirations, fostering a destiny that is not only personally fulfilling but also beneficial to the broader cosmos. This alignment transforms personal faith into a universal virtue, promoting a harmonious, enlightened existence that transcends mere individual achievement and contributes to the collective upliftment of society.

ৡৡৡ

"Change is the only constant in life, a truth embraced by the Gita. With acceptance comes freedom from fear. Approach change as the unfolding of the divine plan, perfect in its timing and its lessons."

❦❦❦

NINETEEN

LIBERATION THROUGH RENUNCIATION

The final chapter of the Bhagavad Gita, Chapter 18, titled "Liberation Through Renunciation," provides a comprehensive conclusion to the spiritual teachings of the scripture, focusing on how renunciation can lead to ultimate freedom, fulfillment, and self-realization. This concept of renunciation is nuanced and profound, involving much more than the mere abandonment of physical possessions; it encompasses a deep relinquishment of egoistic desires and attachments to outcomes, which are seen as the root causes of bondage and suffering.

Renunciation, in the context of the Gita, is primarily about surrendering the ego's control over the will and actions. This surrender is not a sign of weakness or inactivity; rather, it is a powerful state of being that emerges from understanding one's true nature as the soul, separate from the body and mind's desires and aversions. This understanding leads to a form of action that is performed in alignment with one's higher self and the larger cosmic order, free from the personal ego's demands and expectations.

The Gita elaborates that true renunciation is the practice of performing one's duty without attachment to the results. This is often referred to as Karma Yoga, the yoga of selfless action. Here, actions are done not for the sake of personal gain but as an offering to the divine. This shift in perspective changes the nature of action, from being a source of bondage to a means of liberation. By detaching from the fruits of actions, individuals free themselves from the dualities of pleasure and pain, success and failure, which are the main causes of mental disturbance and suffering.

Such renunciation fosters a deep inner peace because it aligns an individual with their dharma (duty), allowing them to act according to their nature and role in life without undue stress or expectation. This alignment ensures that while they are fully engaged in the world, they are not entangled by it. They become like the lotus leaf, which, despite being in water, remains untouched by it.

Krishna asserts that this state of detached engagement is possible through the cultivation of discipline, wisdom, and devotion. Discipline involves controlling the mind and senses to reduce their susceptibility to distractions and temptations. Wisdom is the knowledge of the self and the understanding of the impermanent nature of the material world. Devotion is directed towards the divine, seeing and serving the divine in all beings and actions. Together, these practices help in subduing the ego and fostering a sense of unity with all existence.

Renunciation also leads to fulfillment by liberating individuals from the endless cycle of desires. The Gita teaches that desires are never truly satisfied by attainment, as one desire typically leads to another in a never-ending chain. By renouncing desires, individuals find contentment in what is, appreciating the present moment and their current circumstances, rather than being perpetually dissatisfied chasing after elusive future pleasures or dwelling on past regrets.

Furthermore, the ultimate freedom and self-realization promised by renunciation are described in the Gita as reaching the state of Brahman, the highest universal reality. Self-realization is knowing oneself to be at one with Brahman, beyond the limited identity ascribed to the physical and mental constructs. This realization is the highest goal of human life, bringing with it not only peace and contentment but also a profound understanding of the universe and one's place within it.

Renunciation thus transforms the individual's journey through life. It turns every action into an expression of the divine, every interaction into a reflection of the self, and every moment into an opportunity for spiritual growth. It teaches that freedom is not found in external conditions but in the state of one's mind and heart.

The teachings of the Gita on liberation through renunciation offer a path that leads to deep personal and spiritual development. This path encourages living in the world with a sense of duty, love, and detachment, promoting a life of harmony with oneself and with the universe. By embracing renunciation, individuals are not withdrawing from life but are instead engaging with it more profoundly and meaningfully, achieving a state of freedom and fulfillment that is both liberating and enlightening. This way of being not only enhances one's own life but also uplifts those around them, contributing to a more conscious and compassionate world.

ᐁᐁᐁ

"The Gita's call to selfless action is a remedy for the ailments of the ego. Serve without seeking reward, act without claiming credit. In this selflessness, discover the profound joy of being part of something larger than oneself."

❥❥❥

TWENTY

SUMMARY: EMBRACING LIFE'S JOURNEY

The teachings of the Bhagavad Gita offer a profound and timeless wisdom that is especially relevant to the complex challenges faced by young individuals today. This ancient scripture not only provides spiritual guidance but also practical advice on how to live a life filled with courage, purpose, and wisdom.

The Gita's core teachings encourage an understanding of one's true nature, the development of self-discipline, the importance of duty, and the realization of the interconnectedness of all life.

Understanding One's True Nature

One of the pivotal lessons of the Gita is the distinction between the eternal self and the temporary physical body. The Gita teaches that the true self is the soul (Atman), which is eternal, unchanging, and inherently blissful. Recognizing this helps individuals see beyond the transient nature of physical existence and the fleeting emotions and challenges that come with it.

This understanding fosters a sense of inner stability and peace, empowering young individuals to face life's ups and downs with equanimity.

The Power of Right Action

The Gita emphasizes the importance of Karma Yoga, the path of selfless action, which advocates performing one's duties without attachment to the results. This teaching is crucial in cultivating a sense of duty while also developing detachment.

For young people, this can mean pursuing their ambitions and goals with dedication and effort, but without being overly attached to success or failure. This approach reduces stress and anxiety, enabling them to focus on the process rather than merely the outcomes.

The Role of Discipline

Self-discipline is a recurring theme in the Gita. It speaks to the need for controlling one's mind and senses to lead a balanced and ethical life. For the youth, developing discipline in daily routines, studies, and personal habits can build a strong foundation for lifelong success and fulfillment. Discipline also extends to ethical living and decision-making, ensuring that one's actions are always aligned with dharma (righteousness).

Wisdom Through Self-Reflection

The Gita advocates for Jnana Yoga, the path of knowledge, which involves a deep introspection and understanding of the larger truths of life.

Engaging in regular self-reflection helps young individuals

understand their strengths and weaknesses, their motivations, and their purpose in life. This self-knowledge is vital for personal growth and helps in making choices that are in harmony with their true nature and life goals.

Developing Devotion

Bhakti Yoga, or the path of devotion, is highlighted in the Gita as a powerful means to connect with the divine. It teaches that cultivating a sense of devotion in one's life can transform everyday experiences into spiritual practices. For young people, this can translate into approaching relationships, studies, and even hobbies with passion and reverence, seeing the divine presence in all aspects of life.

The Importance of Equality and Compassion

The Gita teaches that all living beings are manifestations of the same divine essence and should be treated with respect and compassion. This understanding encourages young individuals to embrace diversity, act with empathy, and contribute positively to society. It also fosters a sense of global citizenship and responsibility.

Embracing Change

Finally, the Gita acknowledges that life is full of changes and challenges. It teaches that accepting and embracing change is crucial for personal and spiritual growth. For the youth, this means learning to adapt, being open to new experiences, and being resilient in the face of adversity.

In summary, the Bhagavad Gita provides a comprehensive guide for living a life that is not only personally fulfilling but also beneficial to others. It encourages young readers to live with courage, act with purpose, and seek wisdom.

By integrating these teachings into daily life, young individuals can navigate their journey with a sense of confidence and clarity, contributing to their own well-being and to the greater good of society. Embracing these lessons can help transform challenges into opportunities for growth and lead to a deeper understanding of life's profound beauty and complexity.

❦❦❦

"Let integrity be the foundation of your actions. The Gita teaches that righteousness preserved is destiny fulfilled. Walk the path of integrity, and it will lead you to the ultimate truths of existence."

▷▷▷

Citation And References

This book represents the culmination of extensive research and meticulous analysis, incorporating a diverse range of sources, including numerous books, scholarly studies, and personal experiences. Additionally, I have scoured various websites to gather relevant information and data essential for the compilation of this work. I have taken every precaution to ensure the accuracy of the information presented and have diligently cited all sources to acknowledge their contributions.

Despite these efforts, the possibility of inadvertent errors remains. I deeply value the insights of my readers and appreciate any feedback that can help identify and rectify such inaccuracies. I encourage you to bring any discrepancies to my attention.

Your feedback is not only welcome but crucial, as it will aid in correcting current editions and enhancing the content of future ones. I am committed to maintaining the highest standards of accuracy and reliability in my work and thank you for your support and understanding.

Additionally, I firmly uphold the principle of freedom of speech and expression as guaranteed under Article 19(1)(a) of the Constitution of India, and I respect the diverse viewpoints and expressions of all readers.

ppp

Other Books Of The Author

1. Empowering Minds: A Journey into Women's Self-Discovery and Power
2. The Dynamics of Motivation: Catalyzing Thought into Action
3. Meditation and Mental Well Being: The Path to Inner Peace and Clarity
4. The Psychology of Child Education: Nurturing Future Generations
5. Ethical Enlightenment: A Modern Guide to Living with Integrity
6. Voices of Empowerment: Stories of Women Rising Against Odds
7. Social Psychology in Everyday Life: Understanding Human Connections
8. The Essence of Motivational Speaking: Inspiring Change in Others
9. Balancing Acts: Women, Work, and the Will to Lead
10. Guiding with Grace: Raising Children with Compassion and Awareness
11. The Power of Positive Aging: Embracing Life After Fifty
12. Building Resilient Communities: Social Work in Action
13. The Ethical Educator: Principles for Teaching and Learning
14. From Insight to Impact: Social Psychology for a Better World
15. The Ethics of Empathy: A Guide to Ethical Living
16. The Science of Empowering the Self: Navigating Life's Challenges with Psychological Wisdom
17. The Mindful Conscious Leader: Meditation Techniques for Modern Management
18. Pioneering Spirit: Women's Pathways to Leadership and Empowerment
19. Feeling to Healing: The Role of Emotional Intelligence in Child Development
20. Transformative Talks and Words of Inspiration: Insights into Motivational Oratory

21. The Hidden Path to Ethical Sustainability: Crafting a Greener Tomorrow
22. Spiritual Integrity: Navigating Life with Moral Compassion
23. Clean Living, Clean Society: The Ethics of Cleanliness
24. Patriotic Spirits: Building a Nation on Positive Attitudes
25. Innovative Integrity & Vibrant Visions: The Ethical and Entrepreneurial Spirit of Gujarat
26. Youthful Visions, Endless Possibilities: Inspiring Ethics and Motivation in Children
27. Living Your Legacy: How to Motivate Others by Living Your Values
28. Secret of Healing Conversations: Ethical Practices in Counselling and Therapy
29. Creative Kindness: Crafting a Life of Compassion and Creativity
30. The Power of Appreciation: How Gratitude Can Transform Your Relationships
31. Bhagavad-Gita: Messages
32. Science of Art: The New Frontier of Fashion Modernism
33. Vivekananda's Virtues: A Blueprint for Modern Living
34. Empower Her: Navigating the Path to Women's Entrepreneurship
35. The Boundless Classroom: Innovations in Global Education
36. The Language of Leadership: Communicating with Authenticity and Impact
37. The Warrior's Mantra: Deciphering the Hanuman Chalisa
38. Echoes of Empathy: Transformative Stories of Social Service
39. Artful Living: Cultivating Creativity in Your Daily Routine
40. Finding Your Why: Discovering Your Passions and Charting Your Course
41. The Role of Social Media in Shaping Self-Esteem and Interpersonal Relationships among Adolescents

❦❦❦

Contact

Dr. Minakshi Bansal
Social Activist
Ahmedabad, Gujarat, Bharat
minakshiindiag20@yahoo.com

❦❦❦

|| LOKAHA SAMASTHAHA SUKHINO BHAVANTU ||

• 127 •